Editor: Laura Neutzling
Art Direction: Ron Eddy
Layout: Tod Carter
Illustration: Tod Carter

Published by Big Idea Entertainment, LLC. 320 Billingsly
Court, Suite 30, Franklin, TN 37067

Printed in the U.S.A.

ISBN: 978-7-60587-417-3

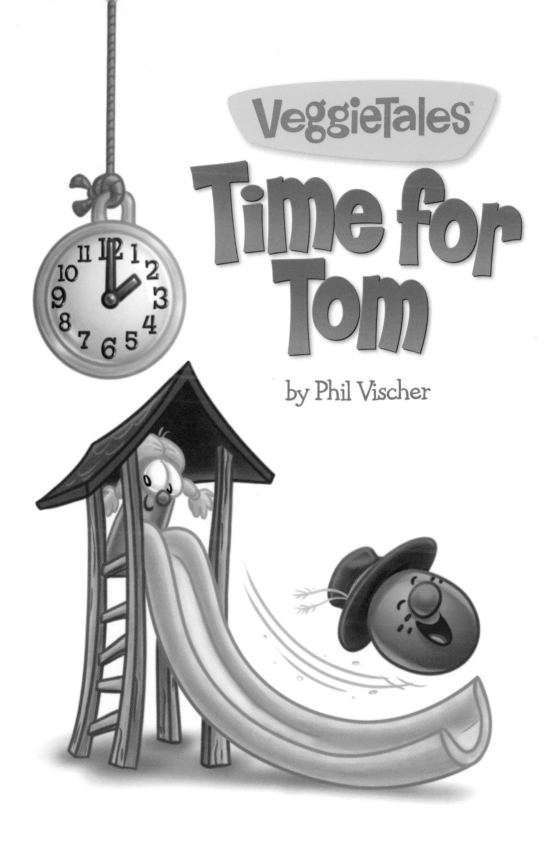

VeggieTales®

Time for Tom

by Phil Vischer

Bob and Larry are here today
To stage for you a little play.
So call your dad and get your mom —
It's time to start "It's Time for Tom!"

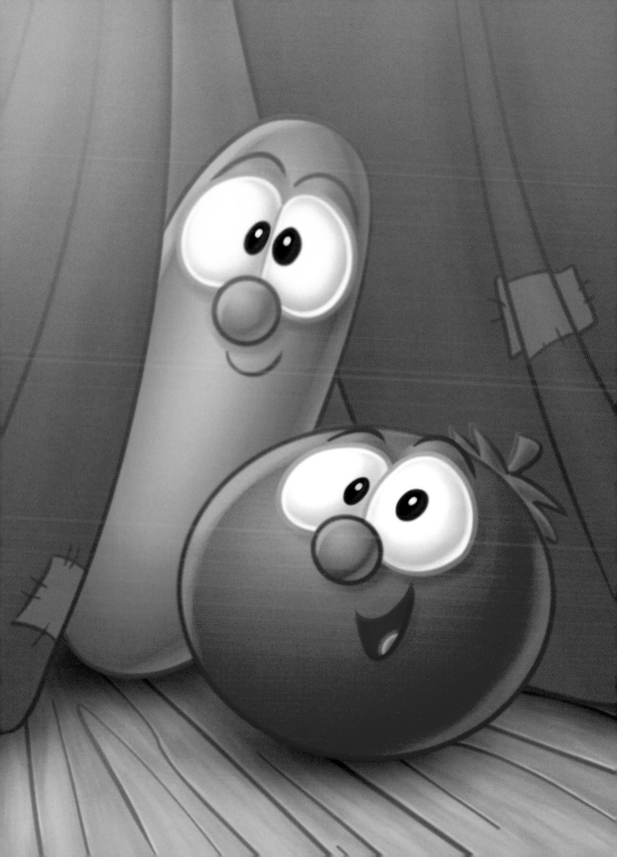

It's time for Tom
to rise and shine.
The sun is up;
he's feeling fine!

The bus will come at five till nine.

It's time for Tom to rise and shine.

It's time for Tom
to make his bed
And fluff the pillow
that holds his head

And smooth the sheet with the
nice blue thread.
It's time for Tom to make his bed.

It's time for Tom
to go to school
And learn about
the golden rule.

And sit at his desk
    on a tiny stool.
It's time for Tom to go to school.

It's time for Tom
to eat his lunch
With Laura and Junior,
his favorite bunch.

With things to drink,
    and things to munch,
It's time for Tom to eat his lunch.

It's time for Tom
to play outside
To run and jump
and swing and slide,

With places for Junior and Laura to hide!
It's time for Tom
to play outside.

It's time for Tom
to eat again,
With Ma and Pa
they sit and then

Thank God for their food
with a big Amen!
It's time for Tom to eat again.

It's time for Tom to hit the tub.
From head to toe,
   he needs a scrub!

So get the soap and start to rub.
It's time for Tom to hit the tub!

It's time for Tom to go to bed.
He's feeling tired —
his eyes are red.

He puts his nightcap on his head.

It's time for Tom to go to bed.

It's time for Tom
to say his prayers.
He's thankful for a God
who cares —

Who fills us up with the love He shares.
It's time for Tom to say his prayers.

It's time for Tom
to say good night.
Pa tucks him in —
turns out the light.

He'll start again when the sun is bright.

It's time for Tom to say good night.

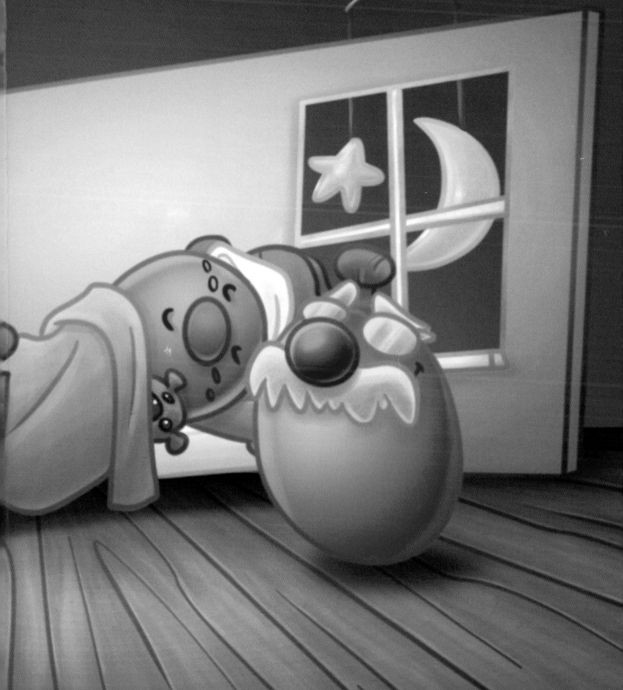

READ AND LEARN WITH BOB & LARRY

This series of Veggiecational Books is designed to help kids learn their letters, numbers, shapes, time and colors! Bob & Larry lead the way with great stories that help preschool kids with their educational basics in a fun and engaging way!

28 page Hardcover books measuring 7" by 9"

A Veggiecational Book about NUMBERS
VeggieTales
How Many Veggies?
by Phil Vischer

A Veggiecational Book about LETTERS
VeggieTales
Bob and Larry's
ABC's
by Phil Vischer

A Veggiecational Book about COLORS
VeggieTales
Junior's Colors
by Phil Vischer

A Veggiecational Book about SHAPES
VeggieTales
Pa Grape's Shapes
by Phil Vischer

A Veggiecational Book about TIME
VeggieTales
Time for Tom
by Phil Vischer

COLLECT THEM ALL!